Don' just do something sit there

Developing children's spiritual awareness

Mary K Stone

RELIGIOUS AND MORAL EDUCATION PRESS

377

Religious and Moral Education Press
An imprint of Chansitor Publications Ltd,
a wholly owned subsidiary of Hymns Ancient and Modern Ltd
St Mary's Works, St Mary's Plain
Norwich, Norfolk NR3 3BH

First published 1992 by S. Martin's College, Lancaster

This edition first published by Religious and Moral Education Press 1995

ISBN 1 85175-105-X

Acknowledgements
The author and publisher would like to thank the St Gabriel's Trust, which funded the first edition of this book (published by the Primary RE Team at S. Martin's College, Lancaster); Quaker Home Service for allowing them to use the title of one of their posters: 'Don't Just Do Something, Sit There!', and the children and staff of Sedburgh Primary School who have demonstrated that the methods described promote reflection and response.

The author is very grateful for the contribution of colleagues in the Primary RE Team of the College for helping her write this book and to Maria Chippendale for typing the manuscript.

Cover design by Topics: The Creative Partnership, Exeter
Cover printed by Ashley House Printing Company, Exeter
Text designed and printed in Great Britain by Sadler's Printers, Wigton, Cumbria

CONTENTS

It is envisaged that this publication becomes a working tool in the hands of the teacher. The author hopes that the ideas will be developed and adapted to suit individual needs.

Section A
INTRODUCTION

A1
Purpose

This booklet has been written to support the work of teachers with regard to pupils' spiritual development. It grew out of a two day course on "Children's Spiritual Development" held at S. Martin's College, Lancaster, in the Summer of 1991.

In writing it we have assumed that teachers and students may be unfamiliar with the approaches described, and intend that this should be a "Beginner's Handbook". Accordingly we have tried to include detailed guidance, to give colleagues confidence to try these methods and begin to develop their own techniques.

A2
Spiritual Development

A significant difficulty for many teachers is to identify what is meant by "spiritual development". Terence Copley has described it as "the development of the awareness that there is something more to life than meets the eye, something more than the material, something more than the obvious, something to wonder at, something to respond to". (1)

If spiritual development, conceived in this way, is embraced as an aim of education (as prescribed by the Education Reform Act, 1988), it is clear that the curriculum cannot be restricted to a collection of assessable activities. The Spiritual is in essence open-ended and undetermined. It is not a matter of "getting right answers".

Opportunities to reflect upon experience, to explore feelings as well as ideas, to develop the imagination as well as the memory, to engage the whole of a child's being in the process of education become important in their own right.

Traditionally, spirituality has been associated with religious faith and for many people it is true to say that their spiritual life is shaped and influenced by deeply held beliefs drawn from a religious tradition.

However, spiritual experience is not restricted to those who count themselves as religious believers. The work of David Hay and the Religious Experience Research Unit at Nottingham surveyed responses to the question, "Have you ever been aware of or influenced by a presence or power, whether you call it God or not, which is different from your everyday self?" Some two-thirds of those questioned responded in the affirmative, revealing, claims Hay, an appreciation of 'otherness' or transcendence as an important factor in human experience.

Spiritual experience, whether or not derived from a religious tradition, is a key factor in the way in which a person sees the whole of life. For this reason, the ideas in this booklet are not confined to R.E. but extend across the whole curriculum.

A3
Aims

In developing children's spiritual awareness our starting point is children's own experience. Our aims must therefore be concerned to help them develop those capacities and skills which will enable them to explore more fully their own feelings and experiences, and those of other people.

Hence

- to develop the skill of being physically still, yet alert;
- to develop the skill of being mentally still, and to be able to concentrate on the present moment;
- to develop the ability to use all one's senses;
- to promote an awareness of and enjoyment in using one's imaginative potential;
- to encourage quiet reflection during a lesson;
- to develop individual self-confidence in expressing inner thoughts in a variety of ways;
- to find an inner peace;
- to appreciate that we arrive at some of our deepest insights through stillness and silence, whether we be Humanists, Christians, Jews, Muslims, Hindus, Buddhists .....
- to appreciate that silence can be a means of communication.

A4

Terminology

Every effort has been made to keep the terminology simple using the minimum of technical phrases.

Stilling is literally "being still" - both physically and mentally. It is used here to describe an activity which offers a variety of methods for acknowledging, exploring and developing the spiritual dimension of life. Stilling develops an inner awareness and values it. It always begins with exercises in self-control, first of the body and then of the mind, and, like all skills, it requires regular practice.

Relaxation is a releasing of all the tensions in the body so that one can sit or lie quite still and yet be fully alert, hence the phrase: "sit in an alert and relaxed position". Relaxation of the body is essential if we are to still the mind. (See footnote).

Visualisation means using one's imagination, whether to recall the shape and size of an object or a situation one has experienced. "Imagine opening your kitchen door and letting in a cat who is miaowing ....." The term has also been used as an abbreviated form of Creative Visualisation, which is when one is led through a story sequence, be it a fairy tale, the life cycle of a leaf, or an experience of a prophet. The person visualising is taking an active role in the story which is told in the present tense, using the imagination to act on the story.

(In other books referred to in the resource list the terms "guided imagery" and "guided fantasy" are often used instead of creative visualisation. Kathy Raban defines guided imagery as "a directed method of tapping the creative, therapeutic and spiritual potentialities of the imagination". (2)).

When muscles are voluntarily relaxed, mental stress dies down too. One can't be angry and relaxed simultaneously.

Relaxation has been found to be successful with over-active and disruptive pupils, and in Sweden it has been introduced as part of the curriculum. There have been reports from other countries too of the beneficial effects of relaxation on learning, health, and the behaviour of children.

*Jane Madders in her book **Relax and be Happy: Techniques for 5 - 18 year olds.** (3) suggests numerous activities to help children to relax their bodies and deal positively with negative feelings. She suggests ways of teaching them to create their own secret happy place in their imaginations whilst they're relaxing, and shows how this method can be used when they want to be calm - when visiting the dentist/hospital, before an exam, going to a new school.*

A5
Cross Curricular
Approaches

As previously indicated, the range of ideas presented in this booklet has an application across the curriculum.

For example, the National Curriculum Council describes mathematics as "a source of delight and wonder, offering pupils intellectual excitement and an appreciation of its essential creativity" (Mathematics Non-statutory Guidance para 2.5).

Maths is typically the pupil's introduction to the concept of infinity, whether in the form of spatial or numerical awareness. As such it raises questions about the boundaries of life and prompts consideration of its transcendent 'otherness', a key function of spiritual development.

Science offers many opportunities to consider the variety of life in the natural world, and can give rise to the sense of mystery and wonder which typifies some types of spiritual insight. Several examples in this booklet concern an approach to the natural world.

The "**response**" **areas of the curriculum** - poetry and literature, music, movement, art, design and drama - invite children to convey feelings, meaning and insights. As such they have potential as vehicles for the expression of children's spiritual growth and also enable children to appreciate other people's experiences. Within RE, itself a "response area", to focus upon spiritual development is to ensure that the subject cannot be confined to an arid concern with external information about religions. The spiritual is about the heart of the subject and leads us to consider the insights and visions of believers.

The links between RE and **PE** regarding relaxation and stilling are dealt with in Jane Madder's useful book (3).

A6

Creating an Appropriate Atmosphere

- a reasonably quiet area or room where you're unlikely to be disturbed;
- where no-one is forced to participate, but where there is always the possibility of joining in part way through without any fuss or disturbance;
- where children can sit or lie down without being too close to their neighbours;
- an atmosphere in which everyone respects the learning experiences.

A7

The Teacher's Role

- to help children value and develop their imaginative powers:-
  - : setting up experiences by using creative visualisation,
  - : valuing the children's feelings, and
  - : giving them time for reflection and expression;
- to explain to children the importance of posture which will help them to be alert and relaxed.
- to ensure that his/her voice is calm and unhurried;
- to provide plenty of opportunities for individual interpretation of the creative visualisations;
- to provide time for debriefing and creative reponses.

A8

Children who don't want to take part

Initially it may be necessary for a certain child or children to be removed from the sight of the rest of the class e.g. in a book corner but within the sight of the teacher. Leave an empty chair nearby with a remark such as:

> "If you feel you can take part later on you can quietly come and sit on this chair and join in. If you find that too difficult just stay quietly where you are. ....."

You're not condoning unacceptable behaviour but at the same time you're ensuring that the child doesn't have to lose face in order to participate at a later stage.

S e c t i o n   B
LEARNING TO BE STILL

B1

Being alert and relaxed

Use instructions like "sit in an alert and relaxed position" at the beginning of every stilling exercise, so that the children know precisely what to do. It becomes part of the ritual.

i)

Turn your chair so that it's facing me and not touching your table/desk.

Sit right back on your chair so that your back is right up against the back of your chair.

Put both feet flat on the floor. (You may need to get smaller/higher chairs for some children, or put a box or some books under their feet).

Place your hands in a cup-like position in your lap, or let them lie loosely on your knees.

Give your shoulders a shrug to make sure you're relaxed even though you're sitting upright.

Now you're sitting in an alert and relaxed position.

With young children this can be made into a game -

"Who can sit right back on their chairs with their feet flat on the floor? Stand up and when I say sit down see if you can sit like that ..."

ii)   While you're sitting in an alert and relaxed position see if you can let your eyelids close very gently ..... while I count 3 (then count 5 then 10 .....).

A count of 3 is sufficient for young children to begin with. Again a game can be made out of closing eyes gently. "Let's see if each group can close their eyes gently .....".

iii)   I wonder whether we can breathe in for four and out for four; in and out through the nose.

         (Teacher:) In, 2, 3, 4.

               Out, 2, 3, 4.

         Now breathe just as slowly by yourself without counting.

iv)   I wonder whether we can put all those things together?

         Can we sit alert and relaxed .....

         With our eyes gently closed .....

         and breathing slowly and gently .....

         until I ask you to stop?

B2
Breathing

Here are two possible ways. Most of the books in the Resources list will give further alternatives.

i)   Sit in an alert and relaxed position .....
Let your eyes gently close .....
Now notice the way your breath enters and leaves your body .....
Listen to your breath .....
Begin counting each slow breath (in your mind). Each time you breathe in count one. When you've counted up to 4 breaths start again .....

If your mind wanders, bring it back gently and start from one again .....

(Pause for a couple of minutes.
With practice this time can be extended).

Now be aware of the hardness of the chair you're sitting on .....
and when you are ready open your eyes and have a good stretch .....

ii) **An exercise that will help children to experience stillness and the focussing of the mind.**

The word 'tightening' may need to be discussed and demonstrated before you begin.

Sit in an alert and relaxed position with your eyes gently closed .....
Tighten your feet by curling your toes under .....
Hold them tense ..... now let them go .....
Tighten the muscles in your legs ..... hold them tight .....
now let them go ..... (repeat this with) -
your bottom muscles .....

    back .....

    shoulders .....

    hands - clenched .....

    neck .....

    face .....

Your whole body has been tightened and now it is all relaxed.
Now take a deep breath and breathe in whatever you need ....
it may be warmth, or comfort, or strength ..... With every breath
breathe in whatever you need ..... (Longer pause).

Now be aware of the hardness of your chair .....
and, when you're ready open your eyes and have a good stretch.

Don't be in a hurry teaching and practising these exercises. It is wise not to proceed further until the children are at ease sitting alert and relaxed, with their eyes gently closed, and breathing slowly and calmly. It may take daily practice for a week or two.

B3
Focussing attention

i) **Using an Imaginary Television Screen**

A few children may experience difficulty in visualising scenes but generally this difficulty disappears if they are asked to use an imaginary television screen.

When the children are sitting alert and relaxed with their eyes gently closed ask them to imagine an empty television screen and use this screen for the visualisation. (This approach has been used with: "The Sea Shore" see Section C3).

ii) **Dealing with Distracting Noises**

(a)   Sit in an alert and relaxed position ..... with your eyes gently closed .....

Listen to all the sounds you can hear outside this room .....
Notice how many there are and whether they're loud or soft .....
Are they far away or quite near .....?

Now listen to the sounds in this room ..... if there are any .....

Now listen to any sounds within yourself .....

Sit very still and listen .....

By this time children and adults are usually quite oblivious to external distractions. Bring them back slowly to the classroom.

or (b)   Sit in an alert and relaxed position ..... with your eyes gently closed .....
Breathe slowly and each time you breathe out feel all the tenseness go out with it .....
Now be aware of you ears .....
Let your ears pick up all the sounds outside this building .....
Now let your ears pick up all the sounds outside this room but in this building .....
Now let your ears pick up all the sounds inside this room .....
Be very still and listen to the sounds inside your ears .....

B4
Using all the Senses

Whether using the imagination in a simple exercise or an extended visualisation one needs to incorporate as many of the senses as possible. It is very easy to think one can rely on 'seeing' alone. If the story is to come alive in the imagination of a child then other senses need to be included:

What noises can you hear? .....
What smells are you aware of? .....
Feel the smoothness of the cats' fur .....

B5
Pauses

Whenever *"......"* is used it indicates a pause, giving children time to enter into the scene the teacher has created. At the end of a visualisation it's helpful if the children have time to comment on the speed of delivery of the story and the length of pauses at each stage. It becomes a learning experience for the teacher!

B6
Creating your own ritual for ending an exercise

This is important so that children know when the imaginative experience has come to an end.
Allow sufficient time to do this slowly and gently.

e.g. We're now going to leave our imaginary visit to -------
and return to the classroom .....
As you sit on your chair feel the hardness of it .....
and when you're ready open your eyes and have a good stretch .....

Having opened their eyes children invariably sit quietly waiting for everyone else to be ready.

B7

Debriefing

This provides an opportunity to explore the children's experiences during creative visualisation.

Sometimes it's felt more appropriate to go straight into a creative activity following the visualisation so that each child's unique experience is expressed, and the more reticient children aren't tempted to copy what other children say in discussion. During a creative activity a teacher has time to speak with each child and value their feelings and the way in which they're being expressed. Whether there is a period for creative activity or not, it's important that the children have the opportunity to discuss their experiences.

When preparing questions to raise with children vary the degree of difficulty needed so that all children can be involved in answering them. Give time for quiet reflection between some questions. Prepare the questions you want to ask before the lesson begins. Encourage children to work in pairs thus ensuring participation by everyone:

There are two types of questions:

Those related to the experience of visualisation, such as:

> **Would anyone like to make a comment about the visualisation?**
> **What did you find easy/hard?**
> **Was there anything particular that you learnt/discovered today?**
> **Was it too short/long? Did I go too fast/slow?** *

And there are more specific questions about the content of the visualisation.

Throughout the discussion the teacher's attitude is one of accepting and affirming all responses. Debriefing is not a test and is not a time to rubbish what is said or pass judgement which results in destroying a child's self esteem.

Many pupils gain confidence from hearing their peers share their feelings and this may enable the reticient children to share theirs too.

---

* *Teachers open themselves to critical comments by the children showing them that it is a shared learning experience and everyone's point of view is welcomed.*

B8
Short, simple practice
exercises

Having taught the children how to sit in an alert and relaxed position with their eyes gently closed the teacher could use the following type of exercise to help children become familiar with and at ease when using their imagination. Begin by getting the children in an alert and relaxed state.

i)   Imagine you're in your kitchen at home .....

You hear a cat miaowing outside the door .....

It may be your cat or a neighbour's .....

In your imagination open the door and let the cat in .....

As it walks past you stroke its back. Be aware of how it feels .....

Because you're being friendly it walks around your feet and ankles and you feel the smoothness and softness of its warm fur against your ankles .....

Watch the cat as it walks around you .....

What colour or colours is it? ..... Is it fully grown or a kitten? .....

Pick up a bottle of milk and pour some in a saucer .....

Then put the saucer on the floor and watch the cat drink the milk .....

Listen to any sounds it makes .....

Now walk across the kitchen and open the door .....

and watch the way in which the cat walks or runs out .....

You're now going to leave the imaginary kitchen and feel the hardness of the chair you are sitting on ..... and when you're ready open your eyes and have a good stretch .....

Other scenes can be created which are based on their homes:

ii) Sitting facing the television: noticing the furniture

its position,

its size and colour

the colour of the walls and curtains

Ask them in their imagination to get up and move a piece of furniture, or look out of the window to watch something.

iii) Having a wash. Turning the hot and cold taps on.
Feeling the temperature of the water.
Using a coloured face cloth.
Splashing cold water on your face.

iv) Hearing someone at the front door; going to open it; seeing who's there and speaking with them.

Other scenes could take place further afield:

v) A walk from home to the shops.

vi) Watching a horse in a field.

NB With each scene remember to incorporate as many of the senses as possible.

Section C.
CREATIVE VISUALISATION

Appreciation of and entering into the Natural World.

One can use a wide variety of natural objects: shells, twigs, conkers and other seeds, fruits, feathers .....

C1

Using Leaves

I'm going to give each of you one tiny part of a tree. It's unique; there's not another one exactly the same in the whole world.

(Teacher shows a leaf)

Yes, it's a leaf, and here are some more.
(Distributes them).
I want you quietly to examine your leaf .....
Get to know it ..... Look at its shape ..... its size .....
Feel its weight ..... first in one hand, then the other .....
Notice the kind of edge the leaf has ..... it might be smooth, or jagged, or torn .....
Notice the veins .....
Examine both sides of the leaf ..... gently feel each surface ..... You might like to feel it against your cheek .....
Notice how many colours there are, or different shades of one colour .....
Notice the patterns in your leaf .....
There may be patterns in the colours or patterns in the veins .....

This leaf - given you by a tree - is unique.
There never has been one exactly like it and there never will be.

Do you know your leaf well enough to recognise it if it was placed with everyone else's leaves on the table?
Good. Put it on the table in front of you.

We're now going to use this powerful gift - our imagination.
Check and see that you're sitting in an alert and relaxed position .....
Gently close your eyes ..... and be aware of your slow steady breathing .....

Imagine you are that leaf .....
Feel what it's like to be that shape .....

that weight .....

those colours .....

You are a leaf on top of a tall tree .....
You're firmly attached to the end of a twig .....
and you're surrounded by thousands of other leaves .....
all slightly different from yourself .....
Feel the gentle wind on both sides of you ..... enjoy the feeling ..... Is it
a warm wind ..... or a cool one?

Now feel the refreshing rain ..... washing you ..... making you shine.....
Listen to the splash of the raindrops as they hit you .....
and listen to the droplets splash off you onto other leaves .....

(You might end here)   Feel the rain ..... refreshing .....
gentle ..... cooling ..... cleansing .....

Go back to the time in the spring when you were a bud .....
Feel what it was like to be tightly closed up, safe and warm .....
Feel the warmth of the spring sunshine making you want to open up
to this outer warmth .....
Feel the life force flowing into you from your twig .....
Very, very slowly you open .....
The tiny leaves within the bud start growing and opening .....
and you are one of these leaves .....
Finally you're fully uncurled ..... facing the sun ..... absorbing
its rays ..... turning your pale greenness into rich bright green .....

All through the summer you live amongst all the other leaves .....
growing ..... feeling the strength of the tree running through your
veins .....
You feel yourself moving in the breeze, light and graceful ..... still
firmly attached to your twig .....
You have felt the sun ..... the wind ..... the rain .....

You are fully grown .....

What's more - you have a marvellous view from your high position on the tree .....

What can you see .....? Have a good look around .....

Can you see the other trees .....? Can you see creatures in the trees? ..... What can you see in the distance? ..... How wonderful to have such a view .....!

Autumn approaches and you feel a difference .....

The strength of the sap surging through your veins ceases .....

You feel yourself drying up .....

Your bright greenness begins to fade .....

But you're aware of new colours appearing on your skin .....

Notice what colours they are ..... brown, or gold or red ..... or a mixture of colours .....

Suddenly, a strong gust of wind blows you completely free from the twig on which you've spent your whole life .....

The wind lifts you ..... You're completely free .....!

The wind carries you high above the trees .....

You twist ..... and turn ..... and float ..... and dance .....

Feel the movement ..... enjoy it .....

Then the wind drops and you float gently down .....

till you rest on other fallen leaves lying on the ground .....

It's very peaceful here .....

What will happen to you now? .....

Do children come and have fun walking through the pile of leaves? ..... Or does some small creature collect you to make itself a warm nest for the winter? .....

Or do you lie quite still, gradually rotting away until you become beautiful dark leaf mould which will feed the soil so that the trees may grow new leaves next spring? .....

Feel what happens to you .....

Now we're going to leave our imaginary life as a leaf and return to the classroom, ... and when we're ready we'll open our eyes and have a good stretch.

This visualisation was used with a Year 6 class who then brainstormed words which expressed their feelings at each stage of the growth as a leaf. This was followed by writing poems which expressed their feelings. They also drew their leaves or the tree on which they had lived their lives.

The Leaf.

Tightly tied up, scrunched into a bud,
Skittish,
Unable to spread out, cramped:
But cosy dozy.
Dreamy and warm

A dazzling brightness
Delightful scents of breezy fresh air,
Energy surging through my veins.
Flowing, swaying, refreshed.
The hustle and bustle of a country of leaves.
An amazing feeling.
Glistening as the sun touches my sides

Dainty, petite as I turn cartwheels in the open air.
Floating weightlessly.
Swiftly descending
Falling onto a bed of scattered leaves
Turning crisp, frail, fainter and fainter
Comfortable, settled, waiting!

Laura

Leaf Adventure

Peacefully sitting there in my tight bud,
feeling warm, safe and secure in my cosy dome.
Crammed in my home,
in total need of a stretch.
Then a crack split open.
I sprang out with glee.
Still attached to the tree,
I gazed with excitement.
I scanned the scene,
Full of contentment
Then I began to get scared of heights.
But I knew I was "Mr World",
I was on top of everything
But not for long!!
My twig broke and I fell.
Faster and faster,
Twisting, twerling, spinning and surging to the ground. Then......
POOFF!!!
I landed under the tree.

I sat up, dazed, after the great fall.

I began to get anxious and I looked around me

I tried to get up but I felt numb.

I began to get nervous.

I didn't know what would happen next.

But at least I was sheltered from the cold.

I was just sitting there.

Deserted

Abandoned.

Worthless

Unwanted

And then, a bird swooped down,

Picked me up and took me to its nest.

Which was under consruction.

Three big oval shapes fell on me

And the last of my life was crushed out of me.............

David

The Leaf

Safe and sound in that little bud
I wish I could stay here I wish I could.
But I am getting too big now
I'm ready for a stretch
I'm all tied in and very very crushed.

But now it has happened now I am free
Amazed of the world around me,
Up in the sky centre attraction,
Ready for action
Shining in the sun up above.

Light and crisp,
Turning cartwheels,
Falling falling down
Unimportant, unadmired,
Dazzled by the wind,
Damp and soggy full of thought.
What is going to happen?

Jessica.

24

The Leaf

Tight and cramed in,
And ready to leap
In need of a stretch
In that dark little heap.

But now I'm adult like
And flowing and brave
but in Autumn,
I'm going to my grave

Now I'm dead
And brown and old
but in no time atall
I'll be lovely leaf mould

David

Space permits only four poems to be included but the quality of work of all the children was impressive after only two or three sessions of this type of work. Here are some snippets from other poems:

"I am alive. Full bright .....
Bullied by the wind"   Vicky

"How long will I be like this?
Oh, how long?"   David A.

"Like a tiny mouse
Squashed in tight."   Kate

"I'm ready to burst,
I need to be brave."   Anon

"All scrunched up
and ready to burst."   Anon

Other responses could include:

Movement - with or without a sound accompaniment.

Painting or sketching one part of the leaf's life.

Followed by an opportunity to share these with others in the class.

Further developments

i) Discussion - **Which part of the visualisation did you most enjoy and why?**
   - **Did all the leaves end up in the same way?**
   - **They all died yet their feelings were different. Why was this, do you think?**
   - **In what way is our life like or unlike that of the leaf?**

ii) Children can learn more about the life cycle of a tree and then write down / discuss what they feel to be the most marvellous aspect, that which fills them with wonder.

iii) Discuss or otherwise respond to poems in:

   The Edge of Wonder (6)

   Threads of Creation (7)

   Leaves from the Tree of Peace (8)

C2

Stones

This work was with 7 year olds.

Each child was given a stone and had to get to know it through its shape, colour, size, texture and weight. They were also asked to examine it from different angles.

Having then placed their stone on the table in front of them they sat in an alert and relaxed position with their eyes closed and imagined the stone with all its characteristics. If there was any part they couldn't remember they opened their eyes, looked at their stone, and then visualised it again.

Following this they were asked to imagine that they had become the stone and were lying on the sea shore, sometimes exposed to the sun and the air and sometimes covered by the sea. They were encouraged to note what they saw and heard and felt, and what kind of an experience it was for them. Then they were brought slowly out of their visualisation.

The Follow-up included a discussion of their feelings and it was interesting to note how many contained both positive and negative feelings. There was also discussion as to what the stones could have done to turn their negative feelings into positive ones.

They drew their stones and wrote an account of their feelings as a stone.

Here's some of their work:

"My stone came from Iona, way up in Scotland. In my feelings I imagine a little hole with lots of stones in and mine on top.
It's smooth and it feels like the wind on my cheek.
I can imagine myself with it in my hand ....
When it's breezy I go under a rock where there is a good shelter. In my feelings I go on adventures ...."

Notice the ease with which the child moves from being the stone, to holding it, and back to being it, without any difficulty.

"I felt smooth like a shell that had come up out of the sea.
I felt happy amongst the other stone.
I felt white and green and red and brown and black.
I could feel the cracks. It was like the sea waves and I felt like a shimmering shell."

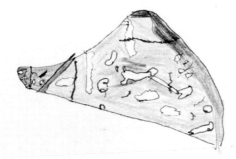

"I felt smooth and happy because the sea had washed me smooth and I could play with the other stones on the beach. I had lots of nice colours in me. I was not lonely because I had lots of friends to play with me.
Then one day someone dropped a stone next to me and I made a new friend right next to me, so that was another nice feeling."

Use can also be made of other scenes in the natural world:

C3
The Sea Shore

Turn on your television and see yourself on the sea shore ..... You notice the colour of the sea and the way in which it moves.....

You look carefully at the shore ..... Is it made of sand, or stones, or a mixture? You make it how you want it to be.

You touch two things that are lying on the shore ....

You look at their shape ..... and colour ..... and size .....and feel their weight ..... then you put them back on the beach.

Now you sit or lie on the beach and listen carefully .....

You see if you can hear two sounds .....

You feel the warmth of the sun on parts of your body .....

You stand up and look around again and enjoy being in this place .....

Now you turn off the television screen and the pictures of the beach disappear ..... You're back in the classroom ..... Take a deep breath and let it out slowly ..... Now open your eyes and have a good stretch.

A variation of this creative visualisation: "Breathing the Waves" can be found in
Stilling: A Pathway for Spiritual Learning in the National Curriculum (4)

C4

a) Creating a Special Place in Nature

This visualisation takes us to a very comfortable and safe place, where we can be completely relaxed. It can help children (and adults) to learn to be still in body and mind, and is very useful in times of stress. If we think angry thoughts we end up acting angrily, but if we think of calm, peaceful situations or people we too become calm.

We're going on an imaginary journey into the countryside.

It may be a place you have visited in real life or it may be an imaginary one. You decide .....

Please sit in an alert and relaxed position ...

Let your eyes close gently ..... Feel relaxed .....

Feel your shoulders drop .....

Be aware of your own slow, regular breathing .....

Now imagine you're in a beautiful field .....

and you walk barefoot across the field feeling the softness of the grass under your feet ..... As you walk you notice the small clouds drifting by and changing shape .....

Feel the warmth of the sun ..... on your face and arms ..... As you walk across the field you see some trees ..... How big are they? ..... How many are there? ..... A few, or many .....?

You can hear the breeze rustling the leaves .....

You can hear the birds twittering in the branches .....

Near the trees there is a stream, and because it's a warm day and you're already barefoot you decide to paddle .....

Feel the coolness of the water on your feet and ankles ..... refreshing them .....

Feel the smoothness of the sand beneath your feet and between your toes .....

You now decide to have a rest ..... You lie on the bank beside the river ..... and rest in the warmth of the sunshine ..... You feel peaceful, ... relaxed ..... and so light you could float .....

Having rested we're going to leave that imaginary place and return to the classroom, and when we're ready we'll open our eyes and have a stretch .....

Debriefing

A time for reflection and response. Three alternatives:

i) a) **With your partner share the part of the visualisation that you most enjoyed or found most interesting.**

b) Class discussion - sharing the paired discussion. Accepting all ideas as of worth.

c) **How do you feel now?**
Did you feel like that before you began?
Did I give you enough time to imagine you were there doing all those things? Or was I too slow?

ii) a) **With your partner note down all the feelings you had**
as you walked across the field,
as you paddled, and
as you relaxed on the bank.

b) Class discussion - sharing ideas.

c) The words/phrases could be noted on the blackboard and used in writing a short poem, e.g. a Haiku.

iii) a) **Paint/draw a picture of the part you most enjoyed.**

b) **Share your feelings with your friends.**

This visualisation could be repeated whenever you felt it would be helpful. It could also be a starting point for the children to create their own special place.

C4

b) My Special Meadow   Here's a different version of the same theme to show how easy it is to adapt an idea.

Sit in an alert and relaxed position .....
Let your eyelids gently close .....
Notice your breathing .....

Imagine that you are in a meadow full of spring flowers .....
You're sitting on the grass at the edge of the meadow near a stream .....
Using all your senses put in the details .....
Feel the grass with your fingers .....
Dip your hand into the stream and feel the movement of the cool water .....
Listen ..... What sounds can you hear? .....
from the water? ..... from the creatures? .....
Is there any wind? .....
Can you feel it on your face? .....
Can you see its effect as it blows across the field? .....
Bend over and smell one of the flowers .....
Know your meadow well .....
by looking ..... by listening ..... by feeling .....
Add things to your meadow so that it's a special place for you to visit whenever you want somewhere beautiful and peaceful .....

Now we're going to leave our own special meadow and return to the classroom. Stretch your fingers ..... Wriggle your toes ... Open your eyes ... and have a good stretch ...

C5
The Raft

This exercise is excellent for relaxing the body and stilling the mind.

Sit in an alert and relaxed position ...
Let your eyes close gently ...
Be aware of your slow, regular breathing ...
Your body is very relaxed ...

Imagine you are lying on a raft which is floating on a lake ...

Feel the gentle ripples of the water flowing under the raft ...
Feel the water supporting you on the raft ...
Whenever thoughts go through your mind pretend they are ripples in the water ... just floating away from you ...

Now your lake is perfectly still ...
There are no ripples ... the lake is still ... (several minutes)

Now we're going to leave our imaginary raft on the lake and return to the classroom ...
Feel the hardness of the chair you're sitting on ...
And when you're ready, open your eyes and have a good stretch ...

Debriefing

Possible questions for reflection and discussion:

i) **What was this experience like for you?**
ii) **Do you feel different now from how you felt before we began?**
iii) **Why do you think this is?**
iv) **Why do you think many religious people have a time of quiet and stilling each day?**

This could lead to a discussion on prayer.

C6

A Visit to a Wise Person Variations on this visualisation may be found in a variety of books. If you use the one in **New Methods in RE Teaching: An Experiential Approach** (5) p.162f. you can vary its length according to the age and experience of the children.

A Year 6 class followed up a shortened version of this visualisation by noting down their answers to certain questions before any discussion took place * Some of their answers are listed under the questions.

     i) **Was the wise person male or female?**

        19 'man'

        3 'woman'

        1 'boy'

        several gave no answer.

     ii) **Was there anything special about the wise person?**

        Many mentioned the eyes as being *bright, sparkling, trusting, twinkling* ...

        Clothes were *long,* and the person was generally *old* ...

     iii) **What question did you ask the wise person?**

        Factual questions eg. *Where am I? What time is it? Who are you?* to other questions *Are you magical? What will I be when I am older? Where is the most beautiful place in the world?*

     iv) **How did you feel when you became a wise person?**

        Important, special, in control, intelligent, responsible, mature, happy, clever, good ...

     v) **What gift did the wise person give you?**

        A number said: *diamond, jewel, ring, necklace, ... but others: - a gift of enchantment, a singing sword, the last dragon's egg, a picture of a beautiful rainbow waterfall with a silver unicorn on it.*

---

* *By asking the children to note down their answers before any discussion took place we prevented them from copying each other.*

vi) **How did you feel about the gift?**

Special, happy, powerful, much adored, excited, protective,
wondering what it was for.

This was followed by asking them to draw a picture of the gift they'd received and to talk about it with their partner.

Then there was a general discussion; a sharing of ideas and how they felt.

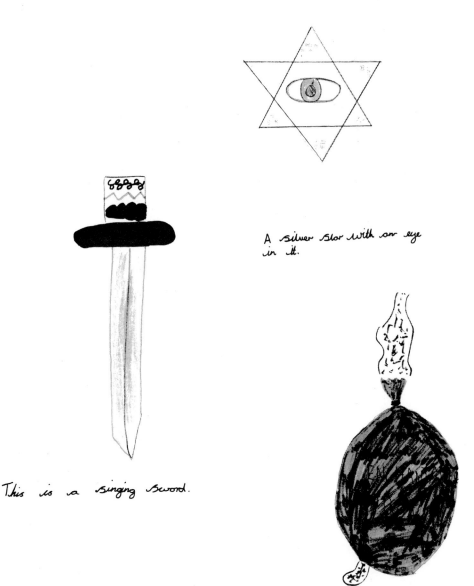

A silver star with an eye in it.

This is a singing sword.

enchantment dust.

C7

Light

This creative visualisation could be used on its own or as an introduction to one or more world faiths.

Sit in an alert and relaxed position .....
Let your eyelids gently close .....
Be aware of your breathing .....

Imagine there's a small ball of light right inside you .....
Now think of it growing bigger and bigger .....
It's spreading to every part of your body .....
The light is flowing to all these parts .....
and taking energy to them all .....
You are full of light .....

Now imagine the light is also outside your body ..... surrounding you ..... warming and soothing .....
You may like to give colour to the light .....
Enjoy the feeling of being full of light .....
and being surrounded by light .....

Now we're going to let the light fade as we return to the classroom, but we'll bring back with us all the feelings we experienced .....

Stretch your fingers .....
and wriggle your toes .....
Open your eyes when you're ready .....
and have a good stretch .....

Debriefing

Discussion between partners, or with the whole class.

- **How did you feel as the light travelled all through your body?**
- **How did it feel to be full of light?**
- **Can you have strong and peaceful feelings at the same time?**
- **Did your light have a colour?**
- **What does your colour mean to you?**

Links may be made with material from sacred texts:

- "I am the Light of the World" (John 8 v.12.)

- "You are the light of the world" (Matthew 5 v. 16.)

  and "Let your light shine before men" (Matthew 5 v.16.)

- "Thy word is a lamp to my feet,
  and a light to my path" (Psalm 119 v. 105.)

- Moses' request: "Please let me see the dazzling light of your presence ..... (Exodus 33 v. 18-23.)

- Arjun's vision of Krishna as his God: "If the light of a thousand suns suddenly rose in the sky, that splendour might be compared to the radiance of the Supreme Spirit. And Arjuna saw in that radiance the whole universe in its variety, standing in a vast unity in the body of the God of gods." (Bhagavad Gita 11/5)

- "God is a lamp of the heavens and the earth, his light is like a niche in which is a lamp, the lamp is glass and the glass like a brilliant star, lit from a blessed tree." (Qur'an 24,35)

- "The firmament is thy salver,
  The sun and moon thy lamps;
  The galaxies and stars are as pearls scattered," (from a hymn of Guru Nanak)

- Reflecting on the importance of light in a variety of creation stories.

Expressing one's feelings   **Express your feelings in colour, pattern, or picture.**
Share what it means to you with your partner.

C8

The Nativity

i) Find out what the children know or think they know about the nativity.

ii) Recap Luke 2 v.7.

iii) Help the children to sit alert and relaxed with their eyes gently closed.

iv) The visualisation:

> In our imagination we're going to visit the stable or cave in which Jesus was born .....
>
> You are standing in the doorway ..... Look around the stable or cave and notice how big it is ..... and what you can see .....
>
> If there's any light, where is it coming from? .....
>
> Is it warm or cold? .....
>
> Who is in the stable? .....
>
> What kind of animals can you see? .....
>
> Listen to any sounds .....
>
> What can you smell? .....
>
> Can you see the baby Jesus? ..... Go a bit nearer if you wish .....
>
> Is he asleep or awake? ..... Is he silent, or crying, or gurgling? .....
>
> If you'd like to hold him in your arms Mary will give him to you .....
>
> If you'd rather watch Mary holding him, that's fine .....
>
> He needs to be held very carefully .....
>
> Can you feel his warmth? ..... Is he awake? ..... Is he smiling at you? ..... or gurgling? ..... or even asleep? .....
>
> Rock him gently in your arms ..... and then carefully give him back to Mary .....
>
> You hear someone enter the stable or cave so you turn to see who it is .....
>
> Go and speak with that person ..... What does the person say? ..... What do you say? .....
>
> And now it's time to leave our imaginary visit to the stable, and to slowly come back to the classroom ..... Wriggle your toes and when you're ready open your eyes and have a good stretch .....

Debriefing

This can be done in a variety of ways. Here are two:

i) Write down what surprised you most during your visit to the stable.

ii) Classroom discussion could follow i) or replace it. Go through the most important questions and ask the class to share their experiences.

In one debriefing session a group of 7-11 year olds shared the following thoughts:

> *"The light was coming from a small lamp"*

> *"Oh, in my stable it was like broad daylight.*
> *The angel Gabriel was standing by the manger*
> *and he was shining so brightly!"*

and again:

> *"When I turned round I saw the inn keeper*
> *standing in the doorway. I asked him why he'd come.*
> *He said, 'I was rather ashamed. I came to see if Mary and Joseph*
> *were alright.'"*

This kind of detail brings the story to life.

When asked how they felt about this imaginary experience their eyes lit up. They felt they had really been there and the unhygienic conditions and lack of warmth startled them into reflecting on homelessness and poverty.

C9

Healing the
Paralysed Man

(Mark 2 vv.1-4 and 11-12)

Read and discuss the story, making the details very clear; eg.

"How did the four friends get the paralysed man onto the roof?

How might they break open the roof?

Would all the debris fall on the people below?" and so on.

Then talk to the children about using their imagination. eg.

One of the marvellous things about using our imagination is that we can travel anywhere we like in a split second. We can also go back or forward in time.

Today, in our imagination, we're going to travel back in time to about 2,000 years ago when Jesus lived in Palestine.

Let us sit in an alert and relaxed position .....

Close your eyes gently .....

Be aware of your breathing .....

You live in Capernaum.

You have heard that Jesus, the great teacher and healer is here, in Capernaum .....

With three friends you decide to visit another friend who is paralysed and unable to walk .....

You arrive at his house ..... What do you say to him? .....

* Notice his expression when you speak .....

* What does he say? .....

You may have to persuade him. If so, how will you do this? ..... Or he may willingly want to go with you .....

What arrangements will you have to make to get him there? .....

As the four of you carry him feel the weight .....

* Listen to what he says as you carry him .....

* How do you reply? .....

When you get to the house it's packed with people.

They're even crowding round the outside of the door trying to see and hear Jesus .....

One of you has an idea and tells the others .....

How does the paralysed man feel? ..... What does he say? .....

Carry him very carefully onto the roof and put him down gently at one side of the roof while the four of you start making a hole big enough to let the paralysed man through.

What do you use to make the hole? .....

As you break it open you hear shouts from below .....

What are they saying? .....

How do you gently let down your friend without hurting or dropping him? .....

* Does he say anything as you're doing this? .....

Having let him down the four of you bend over and look down to see what is happening .....

You notice that everyone except Jesus has pushed back away from underneath the hole so that bits of the roof wouldn't fall on them .....

You watch Jesus ..... Look at his expression .....

* How does he look at your friend? .....

* What does he say to him? .....

* Watch your friend and listen to what he says .....

Watch his face as he looks at and speaks to Jesus .....

You see your friend get up and stand .....

Does he do it quickly or slowly? .....

Does he seem sure that his legs will hold him? .....

How do you know? .....

You quickly come down from the roof and meet your friend outside the house ..... Everyone seems to be talking .....

What are they saying? .....

* Your friend sees you ..... Look at the expression on his face .....

What are his first words to you? .....

As you walk home with him he tells you what happened and how he feels now .....

* Listen and remember what he says .....

You notice how he's walking ..... after all these years .....

* He tells you what a difference being healed is going to make to him .....

Seeing him healed is something you'll never forget .....

And now we're going to leave Palestine and the healed man and his friends and return to our classroom .....

Feel the hardness of your chair under you ..... Wriggle your toes .....

Take a long, slow breath and when you're ready open your eyes and have a good stretch.

Debriefing   Before asking any questions give the children a few moments of quiet while they come back to the present, and time to reflect without any word from you.

Decide on the most appropriate follow-up for you and your class. It may include a discussion of healing - the many forms of healing today and healing in the time of Jesus. Such a discussion should follow the debriefing not precede it.

Here's one possible follow-up:-

i) a) With your neighbour, share the most exciting or surprising part of the visualisation.

b) Provide an opportunity for them to share with the whole class.

and/or ii)   You may wish to go through the happening.

As it's so long choose aspects of particular importance.

These have been marked with asterisks *.

You might end with: "Did Jesus make any difference to this man's life as well as enabling him to walk?"

iii)   Give children the chance to respond in a variety of ways.

Here are two possibilities:

a) Write a poem. It could be a Haiku or something similar eg.

1st line one word	**"Paralysed**
2nd line two words	**Feeling helpless**
3rd line three words	**Unable to walk**
4th line four words	**Meet Jesus. Life anew.**
5th line one word	**Healed!"**

or b) Draw a picture of the healed man.

Show how he feels by what he's doing and his thoughts - in speech bubbles.

Whenever possible give children a choice.

They won't all want to respond in the same way.

C10

Other biblical material

Before using any story the teacher needs to

: think through the questions to be asked, to ensure that they're open-ended,

: include as many of the senses as possible, which entails a great deal of detail.

: the stories used need to make a visual impact.

eg. The Lost Sheep	Luke 15: 4-7
The Lost Coin	Luke 15: 8-10
The Lost Son	Luke 15: 11-32
The Pharisee and the Tax Collector at Prayer	Luke 18: 9-14

Help the children to be present as if they are hearing and seeing what is happening with their own ears and eyes. Use the present tense.

C11

Using Stories from a Variety of World Faiths

Telling the stories in such a way that the children become participants, either as a character in the story or as themselves.

Examples: The founding of the Khalsa, (One could base this on the account in **Baisakhi, (9)**) entering into the feeling of one of the thousands of Sikhs gathered at Anandpur 300 years ago.

The stories of Guru Nanak eg. "The Banquet of Malak Bhago" in **Guru Nanak and the Sikh Gurus** (10).

A part or the whole story of "Abu Ghiyath and the Rich Young Man" in **Stories from the Muslim World** (11).

Other useful titles in the series are:

Stories from the Christian World

Stories from the Hindu World

Stories form the Jewish World

Stories from the Sikh World (11)

Several suitable examples are given in **INSIGHT: Ideas and Practical Suggestions for Religious Education 9-13 (Section E) (12).**

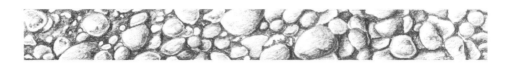

Section D
REFLECTION

D1
Using our senses in a Churchyard

Seven year old children's experiences as they sat quietly in a churchyard. These children had practised stilling exercises for some weeks before this visit.

"In the churchyard I sat very still
I saw some swallows darting in the air,
And the light blue sky shining through the dark green yew trees.
The grey, white and yellow lichen on the gravestones was shining in the sun.
A little breeze blows.
I heard a dove away in a different land and cars going by further and further away.
I felt warm, and I felt that I was in a garden out in the country with flowers all around me"

Adam B.

"In the churchyard I sat very still on the flagstones and looked and listened.
I saw the swallows making patterns in the air, and trying to catch insects.
I saw lots of different colours - green, red, yellow, grey, mauve, , purple, blue, white, gold, and a bit of pink and black.
I heard the birds singing in the air,
There are lots of insects - bees, wasps, flies and beetles.
There was a holiness in the air.
Steven found a holly bush. It was like a secret garden."

David

D2

A Candle Meditation

may provide a meaningful introduction to a topic on Festivals of Light, e.g. Divali, Hanukah and Christmas.

There are several ways of introducing candles. Here are three. *

i) The children sit in a circle facing inwards where they can see a lighted candle.

Watch the candle flame as you sit quite still .....

Just relax and let the candle have all your attention .....

Notice what thoughts come into your mind .....

Follow-up Activity: On strips of flame coloured paper children write down words and phrases that come to them. These may be displayed around a large picture of a candle, and can form the basis of a class discussion.

ii) Light a selection of different sized candles around which the children are seated. Use the instructions as in i)

Discuss:

- **What kind of an experience was this for you?**
- **How did it feel?**
- **What did the candles remind you of?**
- **What differences did you notice among the candles?**
- **Are we like candles in any way?**

iii) Light a candle. After a few minutes of quietly looking at it blow it out and sit for another few minutes before discussing feelings.

Here are some of the thoughts of a Year 4 class in answer to the question: **What thoughts came to you as you watched the candle?**

- *When Guy Fawkes burned down the Houses of Parliament.*
- *Christmas. We have candles then.*
- *A school setting on fire.*
- *Jesus is the Light of the World.*
- *A car crashing - setting on fire.*
- *Going on a walk at night - only a little light.*
- *The olden days when we only had candles.*
- *When the electricity went off.*

** A variety of ways of using candles can be found in **Reflections** (13) and **RE Today Autumn 1989** (14).*

- *The secret seven when they went out at night on bikes to a castle.*
- *Singing carols at night.*
- *It looks like a cross without the horizontal-*
- *When a big boy comes to beat me up.*

When thinking about things that aren't easily communicable children often have ready access to imagery which speaks to them.

In order to work with the children's own experiences the teacher might find it helpful to group the responses and deal with them according to type:-

     eg. darkness and light

         fire

         pleasant experiences

         unpleasant experiences.

Answers to the second question: **What feelings did you have?** included

- peace; peaceful and a bit upset; hot and cold all over; warm; sleepy; tired; joyful; excited because it was alive and flickering; sad; cold, a factory chimney ...

Having accepted and valued all the children's responses the teacher could follow them up by such questions as:
- **What made you think of a car crash?**
- **What made you peaceful and upset?**
- **What made you excited?**
- **What made you bored?**

Children can begin to see how they can feel quite differently about the same experience. They could consider why this might be.

This kind of reflection can prove a valuable preliminary to exploring light as a symbol used in many religions.

(This might be an opportunity for the teacher him/herself to reflect on whether we have a choice about how we see our experience.)

D3
"Sharing Nature with Children"

This book (15) suggests experiences which help children to **feel** the natural rhythm, the changing seasons, and the beauty and mystery of creation. It doesn't set out to teach children **about** nature but to **share** it with children.

These first hand experiences can be used with different age groups. They provide a fund of ideas for creative visualisation:

> **"Be a dandelion parachute, freely drifting"** p31
> **Be a seed germinating and pushing its roots deep down in the soil and its search for the light and warmth above.**

Section E
RESOURCES

(1) MARJON: **Educating for Spiritual Growth** (Video) Guidelines and supporting material for discussion group leaders College of St Mark and St John, Derriford Road, Plymouth PL6 8BH (1989)

(2) Raban, K.F.: **Guided Imagery, Young Children and Religious Education** in: **British Journal of Religious Education**, Vol.10, No.1 (Autumn 1987)

(3) Madders, Jane: **Relax and Be Happy: Techniques for 5-18 Year Olds** Unwin (1987)

(4) Beesley, Michael: **Stilling - A Pathway for Spiritual Learning in the National Curriculum** Salisbury Diocesan Board of Education (1990)

(5) Hammond, John et al: **New Methods in RE Teaching - An Experiential Approach** Oliver and Boyd (1990)

(6) Herbert, C.: **The Edge of Wonder** Church Information Office (1981)

(7) Reardon, J.P. (ed): **Threads of Creation - A Resource Book of Words and Pictures** United Reformed Church, 86 Tavistock Place, London WC1H 9RT (1989)

(8) Reardon J.P. (ed): **Leaves from the Tree of Peace - A Resource Book of Words and Pictures** United Reformed Church, 86 Tavistock Place, London WC1H 9RT (1986)

(9) Cole, W. Owen & Sambhi, Piara Singh: **Baisakhi** Living Festivals Series, RMEP (1986)

(10) Arora, Rajit: **Guru Nanak and the Sikh Gurus** Wayland (1987)

(11) **Stories from the Muslim World, Stories from the Christian World, Stories from the Hindu World, Stories from the Jewish World, Stories from the Sikh World** Macdonald (1987)

(12) Scott, Andrew (ed): **Insight - Ideas and Practical Suggestions for RE 9-13** Somerset Education Centre, 1 Bond Street, Bridgwater TA6 3DN (1989)

(13) Williams, Veronica: **Reflections** CEM (Ref 8917) Christian Education Movement, Publications Department, Royal Buildings, Victoria Street, Derby DE1 1GW (1989)

(14) **RE Today** magazine is included in CEM mailings but can be ordered separately (address above). There are three issues a year. The following articles are particularly useful in developing children's spiritual awareness:
Albans, Phil: **A Fantasy Journey** (Spring 1993)
Hay, David: **The Philosophy of Active Learning** (Spring 1988)
Hodgson, John: **Dreamtime** (Autumn 1990) p.15
Lloyd-Evan, Kathryn: **Religion as Spiritual Awareness** (Summer 1994) p.28
Lynch, Maurice: **Candles** (Autumn 1989)
Scholefield, Lynne: **Listen to Eggshells** (Autumn 1986) p.25
Scott, Andrew: **Stilling - A Pathway to the Spiritual** (Spring 1993) p.28
Stewart, A & Cawthorn, M: **Experiential Learning in the RE Lesson** (Spring 1988)
Waddup, Hazel: **Exploring Sensitive Issues with Infants through Drama** (Spring 1989)
Williams, Veronica: **From Here to Eternity: Symbolic Bridges** (Summer 1993) p.15

Also useful:

Rudge, John: **Religious Education & Spiritual Development** in: **RESOURCE,** Vol.16, No.3 (Summer 1994)

(15) Cornell, Joseph Sharat: **Sharing Nature with Children** Exley Publications (1984)

Other useful books include:

Brown, Alan & Kadodwala, Dilip: **Spiritual Development in the School Curriculum** in: **Teaching World Religions** pp.33-35 Heinemann (1993)

Brown, Clare, Barnfield, Jacqui & Stone, Mary: **Spanner in the Works: Education for Racial Equality and Social Justice** Trentham Books (1990)

Cardwell, Ruth: **Helping Children to Pray** esp. ch.12 Grail Publications (1981)

Culham College Institute: **Eggshells & Thunderbolts** (Video and Teacher's Manual) BBC (1993)

Harris, Maria: **Fantasy: Entrance into Inwardness** in: **British Journal of Religious Education** Vol.10, No.1 (Autumn 1987) pp.8-14

Jones, Alison: **Making RE More Affective** Religious Experience Research Project, Nottingham University (1986)

Hay, David: **Exploring Inner Space** Pelican (1982)

Lamont, G. & Burns, S.: **Values & Visions: Spiritual Development & Global Awareness in the Primary School** Manchester Development Education Project, Manchester Metropolitan University, 801 Wilmslow Road, Didsbury, Manchester M20 8RG (1993)

Macbeth, Jessica: **Moor over Water - Meditation Made Clear with Techniques for Beginners and Initiates** Gateway Books (1990)

Mackley, Joyce: **What is Meant by Spiritual Development and How Can the Secondary School Curriculum Promote It?** (Farmington Fellow) University of Bristol (1993)

de Mello, Anthony: **Sadhana: A Way to God** Doubleday Image Book (1978)

Palmer, S. & Breuilly, E.: **A Tapestry of Tales** Collins Educational (1993)

Priestley, J.G.: **Bible Stories for Classroom and Assembly. The Old Testament** RMEP (1992)

Priestley, J.G.: **Bible Stories for Classroom and Assembly. The New Testament** RMEP (1992)

Rose, J.: **Hindu Story and Symbol** BFSS National RE Centre, West London Institute, Lancaster House, Borough Road, Isleworth TW7 5DU

Rose, J.: **Islamic Story, Folklore and Pattern** BFSS National RE Centre (address above)

Thompson, Penny: **Spirituality and an Experiential Approach to RE** in: **Spectrum** Vol.23, No.2 (Summer 1991) pp.125-136

Wood, Angela & Richardson, Robin: **Inside Stories** Trentham Books (1993)